PECKER DUNNE

LAST OF THE TRA

CW01624012

A PLAY BY TOM O'BRIEN

'I never met Bob Dylan but I sang with Pecker Dunne'
Christy Moore

First printing

Published by tomtom-theatre

PECKER DUNNE – LAST OF THE TRAVELLERS

A play with music about the travelling musicians of Ireland, mostly concentrating on Pecker Dunne and Margaret Barry. They were both from travelling families, Tinkers, and were marginalised by Irish society. Looked down on, indeed persecuted for their way of life. Both were great singers and musicians, and along with the great Johnny Doran, did more to promote Irish traditional music than almost any other person of our times.
Both are dead now and the play is set in a kind of imaginary 'halting site', where departed souls are temporarily resident while awaiting transport to somewhere permanent.

Characters

Pecker Dunne......................40-60 yrs

Margaret Barry...................30-50 yrs

Guard Sergeant.................... 40's

Richard Harris/John Power....50-60yrs

Kathleen.................................early 20's

Johnny Doran..........................late 30's

Mary...mid 20's

Tinker Man..............................30-40 yrs

Step-Mother............................early 40's

Farmer......................................40's

Apart from Pecker and Margaret, all the other characters can be played by one male and one female actor if need be.

Some musicians may be required, possibly a banjo/fiddle player and an accordionist.

Margaret Barry has a pronounced Cork accent, even when singing.

Running time 70 minutes approx

Scene one

A darkened stage, then a spotlight. PECKER DUNNE appears, carrying a banjo case. The case has Pecker Dunne stencilled across the body. Bearded, he wears a wide black leather belt with silver buckle on his trousers, and could be anywhere between 40/60 years of age. He sings I'M THE LAST OF THE TRAVELLIN PEOPLE (c) Pecker Dunne)

PD: Me name it is Paddy, I'm called Pecker Dunne
I walk the road but I never run,
I'm the last of the travellin' people

With me banjo and fiddle I yarn and song,
and sing to people who do me no wrong
But if others despise me I just move along,
and know I'll find friends in the morning
Arah money is money and friends they are friends,
And drinking with them is where all money ends
But it isn't on money it's on them I depend
When friends and the guards are against me.

From Belfast to Wexford from Clare to Tralee,
a town with a pub is a living for me
I haven't a home but thank God I am free,
I'm the last of the travellin' people

The road isn't aisy but it's what I choose,
I'm not always a winner but I'll never lose
I'm the pride of me race, I'm the last of the few,
and I live like my father taught me
Now I'm on the road again travellin' still,
Summer and winter keep travelling I will
But the road it is long and I know it will kill
The last of the travelling people.

As Pecker finishes the stage lights come up. There is a blank screen as backdrop. Towards the front we see what looks to be a travellers halting site; campfire, cooking utensils etc – the impression being given is that the wagons etc are just out of sight. It should be a hazy, sort of unreal-looking place, with a few people seated at various points. Some of these can be musicians.

PD: Where the bloody hell is this place?

On screen we can now read HAPPY 80TH BIRTHDAY PECKER.

PD: Birthday? Eighty? What's goin' on here?

MARGARET BARRY appears from the mist with her banjo. She sings THE GALWAY SHAWL (traditional)

MB:

At Oranmore in the County Galway,
One pleasant evening in the month of May,
I spied a damsel, she was young and handsome
Her beauty fairly took my breath away.

Chorus:
She wore no jewels, nor costly diamonds,
No paint or powder, no, none at all.
But she wore a bonnet with a ribbon on it
And round her shoulder was a Galway Shawl.

We kept on walking, she kept on talking,
'Till her father's cottage came into view.
Says she, "Come in, sir, and meet my father,
And play to please him The Foggy Dew."

She sat me down beside the fire
I could see her father, he was six feet tall.
And soon her mother had the kettle singing
All I could think of was the Galway shawl.

I played The Blackbird and The Stack of Barley
Rodney's Glory and The Foggy Dew
She sang each note like an Irish linnet.
Whilst the tears stood in her eyes of blue.

'Twas early, early, all in the morning,
When I hit the road for old Donegal.
She said goodbye, sir, she cried and kissed me,
And my heart remained with that Galway shawl.

PD: God bless all here tonight. Isn't Margaret great to turn up for my birthday? Ladies and gentlemen, Margaret Barry.

MB: That's the first I heard about any birthday, Pecker. I was told there was a few shillings in it for me.

PD: Ah, g'wan now girl.

MB: Well, seein' as it's yourself Pecker. And it's not as if we're strangers. Shure, we sung together before.

PD: Aye, we did, a long time ago. A chanter supreme, that's what you are. It's me birthday today – apparently. What age do you think I am?

MB: I can still read, boy. (indicates the screen and laughs) Not as ould as me, anyway.

PD: Sure you're no age. If you were six months younger I'd run away with you!

MB: I was born in 1917, boy.

PD: That would make you...ah...
MB: Dead, boy. T'would make me dead. (she looks around) 'Tis a funny auld place, isn't it?
PD: Where is it at all?
MB: There's never anyone around to ask. People just seem to come and go.
PD: It's not a guard station, is it? There's never anyone in them places anymore.
MB: No, they're always too busy hidin' behind hedges and the like to give you a ticket for something or other. Don't talk to me about the guards.

A Garda Sergeant walks into view.

PD: Well, Lord save us, if it isn't auld Baldy Tyres himself!
MB: I know that fella! He stopped me wance in Limerick for havin – how did he put it? – a 'defective rear light on a moving vehicle'. On t'oul caravan, if you don't mind! The lousy fecker.
GS: Well now, what have we here? The Pecker Dunne and Margaret Barry. When did you pair hitch up together? Or is that too delicate a question?
PD: Since when did the matter of delicacy ever bother you? Or any Guard for that matter.
GS: I was only doin' me job.
MB: That's what Cromwell said at Drogheda.
PD: And a lot more places besides. I wonder now if Guards are descendants of Roundheads?
MB: (aside) He have the head of one, anyhow
GS: What was that? (he is walking about, looking at things) You know, you can't park here anymore.
PD: A bit of auld waste ground, on the side of the road – where's the harm?
PS: Ah now, it's not as simple as that. Not like it used to be in the old days. There's the health and safety issue to be considered for a start...
MB: Health and safety, boy? What's that when it's at home? We parked here in 1930, when I was thirteen years old, and we've been parking here on and off ever since.
PS: Not for the past twenty years you haven't. There's new laws these days, official halting sites, proper...
PD: He's talkin' about all these new EU laws, girl. Ah, shure it's all changed since you...since you...(pause) It's the new United States of Europe. We're all only satellites now, being told what to do be some mush in Brussels.
MB: Is that a fact? I'm well out of it then.
PS: Be that as it may. I know you Pecker, and I know what will happen if I give you permission to stay here. There'll be a swarm of you here before you can say 'Ballybunion'.
PD: It's me birthday. I'm entitled to ask a few friends round for me birthday.
PS: Have ye any horses? I don't want any horses roamin' the road – or the farmer's fields for that matter.
PD: Prags? What would a traveller want with a prag these days? The only thing I travel with these days – apart from me four be four – is this. (he waves his banjo case)
PS: I'll be keeping a close eye on all of you. I don't want any trouble now. (he heads off)
MB: He won't go far, boy. He'll be peeping from behind some hedge.

Pecker and Margaret sing DANNY FARRELL (by Pete St John)

I knew Danny Farrell when his football was a can
With his hand-me-downs and Welliers and his sandwiches of bran
But now that pavement peasant is a full grown bitter man
With all the trials and troubles of his travelling people's clan

He's a loser, a boozer, a me and you user
A raider, a trader, a people police hater
So lonely and only, what you'd call a gurrier
Still now, Danny Farrell, he's a man

I knew Danny Farrell when he joined the National School
He was lousy at the Gaelic, they'd call him amadán - a fool
He was brilliant in the toss school by trading objects in the pawn
By the time he was an adult all his charming ways had gone

I knew Danny Farrell when we queued up for the dole
And he tried to hide the loss of pride that eats away the soul
But mending pots and kettles is a trade lost in the past
"There's no hand-out here for tinkers" was the answer when he asked

He's a loser, a boozer, a me and you user
A raider, a trader, a people police hater
So lonely and only, what you'd call a gurrier
Still now, Danny Farrell, he's a man

I still know Danny Farrell, saw him just there yesterday
Taking methylated spirits with some wino's on the quay
Oh, he's forty going on eighty, with his eyes of hope bereft
And he told me this for certain, there's not many of us left

He's a loser, a boozer, a me and you user
A raider, a trader, a people police hater
So lonely and only, what you'd call a gurrier
Still now, Danny Farrell, he's a man

Lights fade, then Spotlight on Margaret Barry

MB: I was born on the first of January 1917 in the city of Cork. Peter Street. Me mother was seventeen years married to me father when she died. I was about twelve then. She was a beautiful woman; I don't think there was a lovelier woman to be got in Cork. Lovely black hair, you know. She used to wear it in a plait right around her head, and all got up in a big bun at the back, with a big

hairpin stuck in it. She got double pneumonia and it killed her. I remember her calling me to her bedside in the hospital and saying 'Margaret, my Margaret'. I never got over her dying. Never. Me father re-married, but I couldn't get on with them, so I set off on me own when I was sixteen and settled in the North of the country.
I sang through the fairs. And the markets. And I had very enjoyable times. And more times it wasn't so nice because there was wind and rain, and I'd get wet coming back on me bicycle from somewhere. But I enjoyed every minute of it. Me heart was delighted when I went through the fairs and could keep on singing all the time. But as soon as ever I'd finish up at some fair or a market I'd actually go to some house. I used to always be hired. They knew me that well. Around Castleblaney, Monaghan, Crossmaglen, Armagh, and all these places. And they used always come along for me and say 'we'd like for you to come up to the house some night, and play a few tunes and sing a few songs'. And there I was, I used to go to the house at eight o clock in the evening and from then until maybe seven in the morning I'd keep on playing for them and singing. I'd get a rest about twelve o clock and get something to ate. And then off I'd go again. I'd play some half sets, and if there was room enough in the place they'd take away the furniture, and they'd dance away the night. It would just be a sociable thing; it wouldn't be a wedding or a wake or anything like that, it was the way they were around them parts, the way they enjoyed themselves. They loved that kind of life you see, the dancing and the craic. It was what they called a house ceili. And naturally enough, it was never without drink. (shakes her head) All gone now, boy.

Margaret sings THE FLOWER OF SWEET STRABANE (traditional)

MB: If I were King of Ireland and all things at my will
I'd roam through all creations new fortunes to find still
And the fortune I would seek the most you all must understand
Is to win the heart of Martha, the flower of sweet Strabane

Her cheeks they are a rosy red, her hair golden brown
And o'er her lily white shoulders it carelessly falls down
She's one of the loveliest creatures of the whole creation planned
And my heart is captivated by the flower of sweet Strabane

If I had you lovely Martha away in Innisowen
Or in some lonesome valley in the wild woods of Tyrone
I would use my whole endeavour and I'd try to work my plan
For to gain my prize and feast my eyes on the flower of sweet Strabane

Oh, I'll go o'er the Lagan down by the steam ships tall
I'm sailing for Amerikay across the briny foam
My boat is bound for Liverpool down by the Isle of Man
So I'll say farewell, God bless you, my flower of sweet Strabane

End of scene.

Pecker and Margaret round the campfire. Others in the background.

MB: Were you ever around Camden in Town the fifties?

PD: I wasn't, Margaret. More's the pity. I was stuck in Manchester. In a factory makin' plastic thing-a-me- jigs. Can you imagine the Pecker in a factory?

MB: I can't. How did you breathe at all? Were you there long?

PD: A few year. I nearly forgot how to play me banjo. It took me months to get back into me stride after I finally escaped. The money was good, but sure that's no consolation for not bein' able to go where you want to.

MB: Freedom, boy, that's all that matters. You would have loved Camden Town then. The Bedford Arms and the Favourite were our meeting places. The finest musicians and singers in Ireland were to be found there at the time. Willie Clancy, Seamus Ennis, Dominic Behan, Luke Kelly to name a few. And of course that's where I met Michael. Michael Gorman. The finest fiddle player of them all...

We hear the fiddle being played; the tune is a jig, THE STRAYAWAY CHILD, which was composed by Margaret. A couple can be seen dancing in the background. The music fades after a while.

PD: The strayaway child. (he hums a bit of it)

MB: You know it then?

PD: Yerra, indeed I played it many's the time on the fiddle. One of Michael's isn't it?

MB: Everyone thinks Michael composed it. But he didn't, it was meself. It was the bane of me life, boy. I spent years trying finish it. I wrote it shortly after I ran away from home, but could never get it right. Michael helped me to put it all together. People were always talking about my relationship with Michael; I mean, they wanted to know was it just musical, or was it personal as well. Well now, I used to say to them, that's between me and the gatepost,

PD: Yarrah, who cares anymore, girl! Sure I was a divil after the women meself. And then after many years I found the one that mattered. Madeline. She gave me a wonderful family. (laughs) She was nearly young enough to be me daughter. But that didn't matter. Shure love bates Bannaher.

MB: And Bannaher bates the devil! – so they say. The thing is, I was never really in love. Would you believe that? Well, I had a husband, but I was only in love with one thing – and that was singing and music.

PD: Ah now...I don't believe that...

MB: I'm telling you. You never met anyone like me, boy – that could say I never loved a man. Only the one thing I'm in love with and that's music.

We hear a woman's voice off

OFF: You're a fraud Maggie Barry.

MB: Who the divil is that?

A woman appears.

MB: Oh Lord save us, it's me step-mother.

WOMAN: Queen of the gypsies me backside! You're not a Tinker – nor a Traveller no more than I am. It's not even your right name. Your father was Charles Power.

MB: It's me stage name. Anyway, my grandmother came from Spain and she was a Romany gypsy. She was a singer too, and played the guitar, and her ancestors was gypsies from Italy.

WOMAN: Don't listen to her, mister. Her father played the music for the silent pictures in Cork for most of his life. He never left the city till the day he died. You can't just decide to become a traveller – you have to be born one.

MB: My people were all travellers. Just because me father choose to stay in Cork for most of his life doesn't change that one bit. What do you know about it anyway?

PD: She's been Margaret Barry all my life. And she has done more for Travelling people and their music than almost anyone else I know. That's good enough for me.

WOMAN: She has you bamboozled, like she bamboozled men all her life. She could always twist men around her finger. Like that Gorman fella, the fiddler, she took up with in London. He left behind a wife and family, broken-hearted and starvin', back home in Sligo.

MB: Why you....! That was nothing to do with me. I didn't even know Michael then. You're spreading malicious gossip. You should be locked up you spiteful auld strap.

WOMAN: Shaa! Anyway, you broke your father's heart when you ran away. And left me to pick up the pieces.

MB: That's your real gripe, isn't it? He didn't want me. And you certainly didn't. You made that clear. It was the happiest day of my life when I got on my bicycle and headed for the North. I was content there for nearly twenty years, living in me caravan, and singing and playing to me heart's content at the fairs and the matches.

WOMAN: Until you ran away with the fiddler Gorman

MB: I never ran away with him. I was invited to London by Alan Lomax to do some recording. That's how I met Michael.

WOMAN: Maybe, maybe not. But you were never a Tinker Margaret Barry. Never a Tinker...(she exits)

MB: And you were always one. By nature anyway. You don't suppose people will think I was a fraud, Pecker?

PD: That's the least of your worries, girl. Sure you're more popular these last years than you ever were when you were...when you ...

MB: When I was alive, boy. Don't be afraid to say it. Well, that's nice to know anyway. (she looks around) You know, I often think this place is a bit like the Wells Fargo Depot. Stagecoaches come in, people get off and get on; they bring a bit of news, and then they go away again. Off to God knows where. And you're left waiting for the next coach to come in...

PD: You're here a long time yourself, girl. Without movin' on, I mean.

MB: Am I, boy? I wonder why that is? Ah shure ours is not to reason why. Ours is just to....well you know what I mean.

Pecker and Margaret both sing a few verses of IT'S NEARLY OVER NOW, AND NOW I'M EASY ((c) Eric Bogle)

BOTH: For nearly sixty years, I've been a Cockie
Of droughts and fires and floods I've lived through plenty
This country's dust and mud have seen my tears and blood
But it's nearly over now, and now I'm easy

I married a fine girl when I was twenty
But she died in giving birth when she was thirty
No flying doctor then, just a gentle old black 'gin
But it's nearly over now, and now I'm easy

She left me with two sons and a daughter
On a bone-dry farm whose soil cried out for water
So my care was rough and ready, but they grew up fine and steady
But it's nearly over now, and now I'm easy

My daughter married young, and went her own way
My sons lie buried by the Burma Railway
So on this land I've made me home, I've carried on alone
But it's nearly over now, and now I'm easy

City folks these days despise the Cockie
Say with subsidies and dole, we've had it easy
But there's no drought or starving stock on a sewered suburban block
But it's nearly over now, and now I'm easy

For nearly sixty years, I've been a Cockie
Of droughts and fires and floods, I've lived through plenty
This country's dust and mud, have seen my tears and blood
But it's nearly over now, and now I'm easy
And now I'm easy

End of scene

PD: My proper name is Paddy Dunne. It was me uncle who said call yourself Pecker. Pecker, that's a great name, boy, he said. And he was right. I think music is something that has got to be born in you. In the blood. Like the blood horse, the drop of blood has to be there. If I hadn't got the music I think I would be very hungry. Nobody else gives a damn for my family only me. All my people were show people, carnival people, still are today. The cinema, fairs, the circus, hurling and football matches, that's where you'll find us, anywhere there's a big crowd

You'd always know spring was here when you saw the crows building their nests, and when you saw the primroses growing at the side of the road, and when you saw me father's caravan coming over the brow of the hill. That's the time when me mother would tell us we 'were goin' off to the country again'.

A man appears in the background. He is dressed in 1940's clothes, the clothes of an artisan, and carrying a set of uileann pipes. He begins to play. The tune is called COLONEL FRASER/RAKISH PADDY. We hear it for a few minutes, and see a couple dancing in the background.

PD: Well, God...do you know what? I'd swear that's Johnny Doran. The great Johnny Doran.

MB: Tis, boy. I'd recognise him anywhere. We were often in competition. At a match, or a fair. If you saw Johnny on the horizon, 'twas time to pack up and move on, because the pennies would be very scarce in your bag that day.

PD: I heard tell of one fair where he collected nearly fourteen pounds for the day's playing - and the wages of a farm labourer at the time was twelve pounds for a whole year. I often collected four or five, but fourteen pounds! (he shakes his head then shouts) Hey, Johnny, is that you? Is that Johnny Doran?

The man looks at him and smiles, then waves. He plays the pipes for a few more minutes , and the couple dance again.

PD: Did you know that in Cromwellian times there was a bounty on pipers? Five pounds, the same as on priests, cos the authorities believed they had the power to incite rebellion.

MB: And why wouldn't they – have the power, I mean - if they could play like Johnny

PD: The finest piper in Ireland. He was one of the Cashs' you know. One of their descendants, anyway. I remember the Cash's when I was growin' up in Wexford. Goin' to school there, and the Cashs' and the Dunnes' being put together on one side of the classroom. That's the way it was for some reason. I suppose it was because we were Travellers.

MB: That was the prejudice, boy. We hadn't a name for it then , we just thought that was the way all people treated travellers. But that's what it was. Pure prejudice.

PD: Because we dared to be different. And it wasn't ignorant people doing it.

MB: Like guards. Or farmers.

PD: It was educated people. Teachers. And priests. The parish priests ran the schools in them days, so suppose it was on their orders that we were...what's the word?

MB: Segregated.

PD: That's the fella.

MB: Like the Jews in Hitler's Germany.

PD: We were in good company then. Segregated be people who weren't fit to lick Johnny Doran's boots.

MD: Johnny would put the heart crossways in you when you listened to him. Did you know he taught Willy Clancy how to play the pipes? Willy himself told me that. (pause) He died young. Too young. He was crushed beneath a wall that fell on his caravan in Dublin. Wasn't I livin' there around the time? Ah, he lived for two year after in a wheelchair, boy, but what sort of a life was that for him? He never played the pipes again.

The music should get louder now, as the couple finish the dance, then disappear.

PD: Well, he's not in the wheelchair now. You know, that's the second miracle I've seen in me life. The first was when a nun talked me into givin' up the lush – the drink. I thought I would never do it. And I told her so. But she wouldn't leave it lie. 'You're an alcoholic', she said to me. I didn't like those words – but she was right. And she persuaded me to join Alcoholics Anonymous.

Pecker stands before his peers, as if at an AA meeting.

PD: Me name is Pecker Dunne and I'm an alcoholic. I had me first drink when I was twelve years old at me Confirmation in Wexford town. I went out to celebrate with my father's brothers who were confirmed on the same day. That was my first drinking session and I went on to drink for the next forty years. I became an alcoholic because I like the taste of the lush. I liked the way it made me feel. I knew at an early age I had a problem but I wasn't able to stop. I tried a few times. I remember coming to Clonmel to play some music and decided there and then to take the Pledge. I managed to stay off the drink for six months; I bought a wagon and horses and felt a lot healthier in meself. But then I hit the bottle again and within a few weeks the wagon, the horses, the nice harness were all gone. I spent everything on the dark stuff in the bottom of the bottle (pause)

I drank everything; beer, spirits, poitin, anything that would make me high. But like many alcoholics I was in denial for years. This despite the fact that I was as bad an alcoholic as you would find anywhere in Ireland. I almost hit a priest once when he told me I was an alcoholic. I was in denial, you see. Drink can strip you of your dignity and leave you with nothing. That is how powerful it is. There are years in my life I can remember very little about. They are like a blur. It is like I wasn't really living. I went through a period of sleeping in graveyards, don't ask me why. I suppose I was in good company because I was half-dead myself. I remember waking up very early in a graveyard in Kerry one morning and thinking, 'God, it must be resurrection day and I am the first up'.

And then I met this nun from Skibereen who saved me. I was in hospital because of the drinking and she came over to me and tried to help me. The abuse I gave that poor woman. 'Leave me alone, I'm dying sick', I would say, But she wouldn't give up. 'We'll have a talk', she'd say. And I would say to her 'If we do have a talk will you leave me alone after that?' And she would say 'No I won't'. Then one day she came over and said 'Now, just relax and listen to me for a moment. Do you know you have a disease called alcoholism? The alcohol is in the bottle and the 'ism' is in you. That's what it is, plain and simple. If you leave the bottle alone you will have no problems. I will take you to a place where you can start to fight your addiction'. And she took me to my first meeting of Alcoholics Anonymous.

When I came out of the meeting she was waiting for me. 'How do you feel now?' she asked me. 'Sister', I said, 'the gates of heaven haven't opened to let me in yet, but the gates of hell are starting to open to let me out'. She put her arms around me and said, 'You know I love you, Pecker'. That fixed it for me. Her telling me she loved me meant everything to me. The drink had brought me so low I didn't care anymore whether I lived or died, but when she said that I knew there was at least one person in the world that cared. I said to myself, 'someone wants me to live'. And shortly after that I met my wife. I've been sober ever since.

Pecker sings the song SULLIVAN'S JOHN (c Pecker Dunne)

PD: Oh Sullivan's John, to the road you've gone
Far away from your native home
You've gone with the tinker's daughter
For along the road to roam
Ah, Sullivan's John you won't stick it long
Till your belly will soon get slack
As you roam the road with a mighty load
And a tooten box on your back

I met Katy Caffrey and a neat baby
All behind on her back strapped on
She had an old ash plant all in her hands
For to drive her donkey on
Enquiring every farmer's house
As along the road she passed,
Oh, where would she get an old pot to mend
And where would she get an ass

There's a hairy ass fair in the County Clare
In a place they call Spancel Hill
Where my brother James got a rap of a hames
And poor Paddy they tried to kill
They loaded him up in an ass and cart
For along the road to go
Oh, bad luck to the day that I went away
To join with the tinker's band

Oh Sullivan's John, to the road you've gone
Far away from your native home
You've gone with the tinker's daughter
For along the road to roam
Ah, Sullivan's John you won't stick it long

Till your belly will soon get slack
As you roam the road with a mighty load
And a tooten box on your back

MB: That's a great song, Pecker.

PD: I wrote that song when I was eleven. And I think it's the best one I ever wrote. It was a romantic incident that I saw among the travelling people that inspired me. We pulled in off the drag – the road – one evening outside Kilrush, joining a camp that was already set up. We were there for a few days and every evening I noticed this farmer's son coming down to the molly – the camp – and he had his eye on this beautiful traveller girl. You could see that that he was crazy about her and she about him. In the heel of the hunt, they were so mad about each other that they ran away to England together. Johnny Sullivan was the boy's name and I named the song after him. He joined the travelling life in England and started his own tarmac and trucking business there. In the song I pretended that he was a tinker tramping the road, but in reality he became a very wealthy man. Ah, that's what they call poetic licence I suppose.

End of scene

A campfire. Singing and dancing. Pecker, wearing a hat is seated, drinking and enjoying himself. A red-haired girl, throws herself down beside Pecker. Soon they are laughing and cuddling..

PD: What's your name?

MARY: Me name's Mary. What's yours?

PD: Arra, you can call me anything, so long as it's not too early in the morning.

MARY: I like your hat. Where did you get it?

PD: Well, I'll tell you now; I was buskin' over in Dingle a few days ago and this fella said to me 'I'll give you two euros if you play a good tune for me', so I said 'give me four and I'll play a better one'. I did, and he was so happy he said 'play me another one now and I'll give you me hat'. I did, and now I'm wearing it. 'That's a good hat now, look after it', he said, 'I paid 140 dollars for that hat in Australia'

MARY: Are you goin' to wear it to Puck Fair?

PD: Begod I am. They might crown me King of The Fair tomorrow with that hat on me head. (the girl laughs, and Pecker says in an aside) I think I'm alright here.

MARY: Will you give me a dance at the fair?

PD: I surely will. I'll even give you two for good measure. (he drags her to her feet) We'll have a practice one now.

They dance close together for a moment. Suddenly there is a roar and a man jumps between them and shoves them apart.

MAN: That's my wife, stranger. What do you say to that?

PD: A careless man and his wife are soon parted, that's what I say. She needs controlling, man.

MAN: Well, if she does itself, I'm the one to do it.

He drags the girl away and shoves her to one side, then kicks out at Pecker and knocks him to the ground. Then he takes off his shirt and stands in the pose of a fighter, his bare fists raised. Someone shouts 'clear a space' as Pecker rises and takes off his shirt. He, too, raises his fists. They circle each other for a while, throwing punches and missing. Then Pecker connects with a wild swing to the head. His opponent goes down, pole-axed. He lays there not moving; someone comes up and tests for a pulse at the side of his neck.

MAN: There's no pulse. I think he's dead.

Pandemonium on the site for a few minutes. Screams and shouting. Then a police whistle is heard. A Guard Sergeant marches on and drags Pecker off.

Lights dim, then we see Pecker singing PORTLAOISE GAOL (c Pecker Dunne)

PD:

For thirty years I've been a tinker,
I've tramped the mountain and the glen I've courted girls in every county,
and I've fought the very best of men
I drank an awful lot of porter, I slept in sunshine, snow and gale
But the life I loved was taken from me, when I spent two years in Portlaoise gaol.

Portlaoise gaol it was tamed the tiger - try, me boys, to get bail
T'was many a heart was stopped inside – inside the walls of Portlaoise gaol.

I joined a camp outside Kilorglin, the night before they crowned the king
There was song and dance and plenty porter,
with our wagons formed around the ring
Then a foxy lass sat down beside me, bedad says I, I'm alright here
But her husband rose and leapt between us,
and knocked me down with a kick in the ear
I hit him hard below the navel,, he hit the ground with a might wail
His neck was broke, he died in seconds,
and I spent Puck Fair in Portlaoise gaol.

Portlaoise gaol it was tamed the tiger - try, me boys, to get bail
T'was many a heart was stopped inside – inside the walls of Portlaoise gaol.

End of scene

The campsite. A man, a local farmer comes into view, in a temper.

MAN: Hey, ya pikey bastard, did you steal that bit of lead off the roof of my cowhouse the other day?

PD: I've been passing this way the last twenty years and the devil a bit of lead I ever saw on that roof. A few galvanised sheets, and they fallin down with the rust, but no lead.

MAN: I'll call the Guards. I'll get you moved on.

PD: They won't find any lead here.

MAN: Well, if it wasn't you it was them friends of your in that transit van.

PD: They weren't friends of mine, whoever they were.

MAN: Well they were over from Rathkeale way then. That town is full of pikeys and knackers. They sold my wife a roll of carpet and when she unrolled it there was a big square missing in the middle.

PD: More fool her then. Is that what this is about? Someone sold your wife dodgy bit of carpet and you blame me for it. How do you know they were travellers? Maybe they were townies.

MAN: They were pikeys. Just like you.

PD: That's not a very nice word. We're travelling people, not pikeys.

MAN: Well you're all tarred with the same brush, aren't you? Steal anything that's not nailed down, you lot would.

PD: Even invisible lead. How would it be if I called you a sod-buster or a cockie, or something else derogatory.

MAN: Look, why don't up sticks and just head off. You know you're not wanted around here.

PD: It's still a free country – I think

. He sings a few verses from **THE TRAVELLING PEOPLE ((c) Ewan McColl)**

PD: I'm a freeborn man of the travelling people
Got no fixed abode with nomads I am numbered
Country lanes and bye ways were always my ways
I never fancied being lumbered

Well we knew the woods and all the resting places
The small birds sang when winter time was over
Then we'd pack our load and be on the road
They were good old times for the rover

In the open ground where a man could linger
Stay a week or two for time was not your master
Then away you'd jog with your horse and dog
Nice and easy no need to go faster

And sometimes you'd meet up with other travellers
Hear the news or else swop family information
At the country fairs we'd be meeting there
All the people of the travelling nation

I've made willow creels and the heather besoms
And I've even done some begging and some hawkin'
And I've lain there spent rapped up in my tent
And I've listened to the old folks talking

All you freeborn men of the travelling people
Every tinker rolling stone and gypsy rover
Winds of change are blowing old ways are going
Your travelling days will soon be over

I'm a freeborn man of the travelling people
Got no fixed abode with nomads I am numbered
Country lanes and bye ways were always my ways
I never fancied being lumbered

End of scene

The screen is now showing scenes from the film TROJAN EDDIE. A middle aged man appears; it is RICHARD HARRIS, playing the character of John Power in Trojan Eddie.

RH: I'm croakin' for some lush, Pecker.

PD: Who's that?

RH: You know me well, Pecker. Didn't you teach me the cant in that godforsaken hole we spent several weeks in.

PD: (recognising him) Well, holy God, it's Richard Harris himself! The last time we met - the only time we met – was on the set of the fillum Trojan Eddie.

RH: That's the place I'm talking about – that God forsaken hole. Twas worse than a real halting site

PD: 'Twas a real one (laughs) What are you doing here?

RH: The same as yourself, man.

PD: (nodding) Passing through then. You're dying for a drink?

RH: That's what I said. Croakin' for a lush. (smiles) Your tuition wasn't in vain. I still remember the whids-

PD: Aye, the words. The parlay chanter.

RH: Listen to this. The Seids – the guards. The tohbar –the road. A mush- a man. A raki- a girl.

PD: Fair play to ya. You didn't forget. Here (he hands him a bottle of Guinness) That's the Buskers Chanter I taught you, a type of parley spoken by travelling musicians and entertainers. There's lots of different variations. Ah, it's all died out now; no one uses it anymore. Mores the pity.

RH: Well, I still remember it. Here's to you, Pecker Dunne, parley poet and chanter. (they drink) Did you ever watch the film after it was made.

PD: I did. I even have a video of it. You and Stephen Rea. John Power and Trojan Eddie. And the girl...what was her name?

RH: Kathleen.

PD: Kathleen, yes. Beauty and the beast.

RH: Steady now. I wasn't that fucken ugly!

PD: Sure you were too old for her any road

As they speak we see a scene at a travellers halt. Kathleen, a young girl appears. In her 20's, she is very beautiful. Richard becomes John Power.

RH: Kathleen! Come here till I show you something. This is where we used to stop. When we were on the road with me father. Right across here. Let the horses off and pitched our camp. With our little wagon on that hill right there. Fresh water, and –look – lashings of firewood for the fire. Meself and me sister Bridget, running through the woods. And those rocks there – see? – we were always climbing them.

K: But you settled down, became part of the settled community.

RH: But I was never a townie. (pause) Ah, I started rambling into the town, knocking around with a few local lads, old billiards halls and that. Then my sister Bridget met a settled boy – and ran off and got married. That sort of finished me on the road too. That summer when my father moved on I refused to go, and they went off without me. I never took to the road again.

K: (coming close to him) But you married a traveller?

RH: Aye. I married a traveller. Kitty. The Lord be good to her. You remind me a lot of her.

K: Was she beautiful?

RH: Yes. She was beautiful.

K: They say you're the wealthiest man in the county.

RH: Ah, money! All the money in the world doesn't buy you more than a shave at the end of the day.

K: 'Twould make me happy. That, and a place to call home. (she looks around at the squalor) I don't like the road meself. When I get married I'm wanting to live in a house. Bit of an orchard at the back and a swing for the children and all. (she looks at John) People think travellers don't like beautiful things but we do. And they think we don't like the cold as well, but that's not true either. (she links her arm in John's) You'll look after me, won't you John?

Margaret appears and sings SHE WALKED THROUGH THE FAIR (traditional)

MB: My young love said to me "My mother won't mind
And my father won't slight you for your lack of kind"
And she stepped away from me and this she did say,
"It will not be long, love, till our wedding day"

She stepped away from me, and she went thro' the fair.
And fondly I watched her move here and move there.
And then she went homeward with one star awake,
As the swan in the evening moves over the lake.

Last night she came to me, she came softly in,
So softly she came that her feet made no din.
And she laid her hand on me, and this she did say
"It will not be long love, till our wedding day"

PD: She saw you coming a mile off, boy.

RH: Sure I know that. But where would I get another chance of a fine woman like that in my lifetime? Me, a tinker gone bad. And nothing but a big empty house to go home to every night.

PD: Aye, you're right. More power to your elbow John.

RH: It's not my elbow that needs the power, boy!

PD: Is that why she ran away with your nephew Dermot on your wedding night?

RH: You know how it is with young girls, their heads are easily turned.

PD: And the suitcase of money she took with her?

The screen shows Trojan Eddie giving her the suitcase and Dermot in the background, watching.

RH: 'Twas her own. Her dowry.

PD: Yerra, I know that. Was she worth it?

RH: She came back, didn't she?

PD: How much was in the suitcase?

RH: Eleven thousand.

PD: Which she brought back, of course.

RH: You know she didn't. Her family, the McDonaghs, they had that away. Mind you, we broke a few heads. We got our money's worth, by Christ, anyway

The screen now shows Eddie finding the suitcase under his friend's bed.

PD: And Trojan Eddie?

RH: The Trojan eejit you mean! Sure I bankrolled him most of his life. Without me he'd have starved – him and his family. If he had brains he'd be dangerous.

As he speaks we see Trojan Eddie on screen, doing his spiel, selling his wares.

TE: What you want I got. And if you can get it cheaper anywhere else then I want to know about it. Trojan Eddies the name, bargain-zinies the game. A walkman? I got it! A razor? I got it! A guitar? I got it! A keyboard? I had one last week. Too late. So listen, don't be done out of it, get down here now. Trojan Eddie's of William Street. Now. (a close up shot of him on the screen) What are yeh doin' sitting there? I said now! (the film ends)

PD: Seems to be doin' alright for himself now, out on his own. A brand new store. And lashings of stock for sale. What did he have when he worked for you, John? An auld van and a stall be the side of the road. And sellin' stuff you wouldn't give to a charity shop. I wonder where he got the money to start up on his own.....?

RH: What are yeh sayin'?

PD: I'm thinking the quare wan wasn't the only one to see you comin'

RH: It's not my money, if that's what you think.

PD: Him and Dermot were very close though. Like brothers in fact. Maybe the McDonaghs were only the scapegoats in all this.

RH: That bloody townie doesn't know his elbow from his instep. Shure he won't pay for any of that stuff. It'll all fall down around his ears before long. You mark my words. Then he'll be crawlin back to me looking for help. Cos he don't stand a chance without me. He haven't got a hope in hell. You see I know who I am, and what I am, and what I am worth. But him, he hasn't got a clue, not an idea. He'll come crawling back on his belly, boy. Just like the woman did. You wait and see. Trojan Eddie! Trojan fuckin' eejit! (by now he is shouting)

PD: I suppose you are right, John.

We see Kathleen in the background, calling to John

K: John. Your tea is ready.

RH: Right, Kathleen, I'll be there in a minute.

PD: She who must be obeyed

RH: She's pregnant you know. Our first child. Isn't it well for me boy? (he goes)

PD: Fair play to yeh John. (shakes his head as John disappears)

Margaret and Pecker watch as John walks away.

PD: No fool like an ould fool.

MB: He was an outsider, wasn't he...Trojan Eddie, the townie?

PD: They both were. Eddie and John. That's what I liked about the film. It showed what it was like to be an outsider from both sides. Eddie , a townie , because he was working and making his living from John and the travelling community. And John, a traveller, who was living amongst the settled community, and had made his fortune as a result. Both were despised in their different ways. (a pause)
That's where the music helps. Woody Guthrie was an outsider. He used his music to challenge things. I'm an outsider too. I use my music and my songs to challenge people in Ireland about the way Travellers are treated. I've also used it to celebrate the richness of Traveller music and Traveller culture. The first people to play the banjo were outsiders to America. They were the black slaves that were dragged halfway across the world from Africa to the cotton plantations of the American south.

Pecker and Margaret sings a verse of Woody Guthrie's LONESOME VALLEY (c) Woody Guthrie)

There's a road that leads to glory
Through a valley far away,
Nobody else can walk it for you,
They can only point the way.

You gotta walk that lonesome valley,
You gotta walk it by yourself,
Nobody here can walk it for you,
You gotta walk it by yourself.

PD: There's a freedom, there is wildness, and there's a sense of pain in Travellers style of music. When you're downtrodden all your life it gets in your chest and it affects you. And it comes out in your music. I can hear that in Woody. Just as I can hear it in you. Did you feel an outsider Margaret?

MB: All me life, boy. But I didn't let that stop me. It was the singing I cared for. Only the singing. If I hadn't had that, what would I have done? Maybe I might'a been a factory girl.

Margaret sings THE FACTORY GIRL (traditional)

As I went out walking one fine summer morning,
The birds in the bushes did whistle and sing
The lads and the lasses in couples were courtin'
Going back to the factory their work to begin

He spied one among them, she was fairer then many,
Her cheeks like the red rose that blooms in the spring,
Her hair like the lily that grows in yon' valley
She was only a hard-working factory girl

He said soft beside her, more closely to view her
She said "My young man, don't stare me so,
I gold in my pocket, and silver as well,
no more will I answer that factory call..."

Pecker appears with his banjo case. He opens the case, takes out his banjo and strums it for a moment.

PD: The thing I love about the banjo is that it's the instrument of the outsider. Me father wanted me to be a fiddle player, like himself. I think it broke his heart when I choose the banjo instead. I got my first one in Castlecomer Co Kilkenny when I was little more than a child. We had gone into a harness shop to get some gear for one of our horses and the man pulled out this dusty old banjo from somewhere and gave it to me. There are times in your life - moments when you feel something was planned for you by the man above. As soon as I held that banjo in my hands I knew we were going to spend our lives making special music together. (pause) And so we did.

Pecker looks at his surroundings for a while then shakes his head. He gathers his banjo and case etc and begins to move away. The light gradually fades and we move to a centre spotlight.

Peckers sings **WEXFORD TOWN** (c Pecker Dunne)

PD: My family lived in Wexford town, stopped travelling and settled down,
Though my father kept a horse and car, we lived within the town,
The people there misunderstood, or they did not know our ways,
So with horse and car, back on the road, I began my travelling days

My father was called the Fiddler Dunne, and I'm a fiddler too,
But although I often felt his fist, he taught me all he knew,
I know I'll never be as good, and yet I feel no shame,
For the other things my father taught, I am proud to bear his name.

He taught me pride and how to live, though the road is hard and long,
And how a man will never starve, with a banjo, fiddle or song,
And how to fight for what I own, and what I know is right,
And how to camp beside a ditch on a stormy winter's night.

O times were good and times were bad, and people cruel and kind,
But what I learned of people then, has stayed within my mind,
I'll honour friends with all my heart, do for them all I can,
But I've learnt to go the road again, when they spurn the tinker man.

O Wexford is a town I like, but the travelling man they scorn,
And a man must feel affection for the town where he was born,
I know one day, that I'll go back, when my travelling days are done,
And people will begin to wonder, what has happened to the Pecker Dunne.

The rest of the cast come out as Pecker finishes the last verse

End (c) Tom O'Brien

<u>SONG LIST</u>

I'M THE LAST OF THE TRAVELLIN' PEOPLE (c Pecker Dunne)

THE GALWAY SHAWL (traditional)

DANNY FARRELL (c PETE ST JOHN)

THE FLOWER OF SWEET STRABANE (traditional)

IT'S NEARLY OVER NOW (c Eric Bogle)

SULLIVAN'S JOHN (c Pecker Dunne)

PORTLAOISE GOAL (c Pecker Dunne)

THE TRAVELLING PEOPLE (c Ewan McColl)

SHE WALKED THROUGH THE FAIR (traditional)

LONESOME VALLEY (c Woody Guthrie)

FACTORY GIRL (traditional)

WEXFORD TOWN (c Pecker Dunne)

<u>There are also two instrumental tunes</u>

COLONEL FRAZER/RAKISH PADDY (traditional)

THE STRAYAWAY CHILD (c Margaret Barry)

Poem For The Pecker (Dunne)

Gather round this cold night by the campfire,and i'll tell you a Tinkermans' tale,
All about a great singer of Ireland,who triumphed where many have failed.
Born into a nomadic lifestyle,a horse drawn trailer it was his abode,
And he travelled the lanes of ould Ireland,and he travelled the dusty old roads.

"Sullivans John" to the road you have gone,Pecker Dunne wrote at eleven years young
And that was the dawn of his music career,and his wonderful story begun.
For he travelled the byways and highways,and could be found on a bright sunny day,
Playing songs down at Croke of the travelling folk,at the games of the old G.A.A

Well he sang of the Myxomatosis and he told of the ould Morris van,
And the tale of the Thirty foot trailer,and the songs of the travelling man.
And he gave us the songs of his people,where others had feared for to speak,
And he spoke out 'gainst discrimination,and equal rights for his people did seek.

Well you'd find him not far from O'Callaghans Mills,in the famed banner county of Clare,
Down among all the horses and trailers at the world famous Spancil Hill fair.
And you'd find him out west into Galway and on the road up to Ballinasloe,
With his banjo and fiddle always close by at hand,for he always would put on a show.

Pecker drank with the great Richard Harris,a world renowned actor and drinker,
And starred in "The Good,Bad & Ugly",not bad for an old Wexford Tinker!!
And he knew Eli Wallach and Oliver Reed,and he acted with the man Stephen Rea,
But he never denied that great traveller pride,on the open road Peckers' heart lay.

Christy Moore never met with Bob Dylan,but he sang with the great Pecker Dunne,
So won't you come now to me little daughter,won't you come now to me little son.
For Pecker played with those brothers The Fureys,and Luke Kellys' own Dubliners' band,
With his own unique style that old banjo he played,and the greatest respect did command.

So always remember his music,and never then forget his face,
For he brought such joy unto his people,and he brought such pride unto his race.
For we are the Romany people,and in that we should suffer no shame,
Dunne,Barrett,Ward or other,travelling sister or brother,you should always take pride in your name.

So farewell to the tent and the trailer,and farewell to the old caravan,
And join me in praise of the great Pecker Dunne,of the Legend,Musician and Man.
For he shall be forever remembered,and his name it shall always live long,
Carried on by the travellers of Ireland,in their poems and in story and song.

AUTHOR'S BIOGRAPHY

Tom O'Brien is a native of Kilmacthomas Co Waterford and is a full time writer, playwright and poet.
Performed plays include **Money from America, Cricklewood Cowboys, On Raglan Road**. **Johnjo, Gorgeous Gaels, Brendan Behan's Women Down Bottle Alley, No Blacks, No Dogs, No Poles,** etc
Books include **Letters To Mother and Other Dead Relatives, Cricklewood Cowboys, The Shiny Red Honda, The Missing Postman and Other Stories,** etc

His two collections of poetry - **'67'** and**'67+'** - are available online. www.amazon.co.uk
All his books are available on http://www.amazon.co.uk/Tom-OBrien/e/B0034OIGOQ/ref=sr_tc_2_0?qid=1388083522&sr=1-2-ent

Website: http://gorgeousgael.com/

https://twitter.com/gorgeousgael

https://www.facebook.com/#!/tom.obrien.5851

Tom has lived in Hastings UK since 2000.

Printed in Great Britain
by Amazon

65266809R00018